Spend Spend Spend

A musical

Book and lyrics by
Steve Brown and Justin Greene

Music by Steve Brown

Based on the book by
Viv Nicholson and Stephen Smith

WWW.SAMUELFRENCH.CO.UK
WWW.SAMUELFRENCH.COM

Copyright © 2003 by Steve Brown, Justin Greene, Vivian Nicholson and Stephen Smith
All Rights Reserved

SPEND SPEND SPEND is fully protected under the copyright laws of the British Commonwealth, including Canada, the United States of America, and all other countries of the Copyright Union. All rights, including professional and amateur stage productions, recitation, lecturing, public reading, motion picture, radio broadcasting, television and the rights of translation into foreign languages are strictly reserved.

ISBN 978-0-573-08121-7

www.samuelfrench.co.uk
www.samuelfrench.com

FOR AMATEUR PRODUCTION ENQUIRIES

UNITED KINGDOM AND WORLD EXCLUDING NORTH AMERICA

plays@SamuelFrench-London.co.uk

020 7255 4302/01

Each title is subject to availability from Samuel French, depending upon country of performance.

CAUTION: Professional and amateur producers are hereby warned that SPEND SPEND SPEND is subject to a licensing fee. Publication of this play does not imply availability for performance. Both amateurs and professionals considering a production are strongly advised to apply to the appropriate agent before starting rehearsals, advertising, or booking a theatre. A licensing fee must be paid whether the title is presented for charity or gain and whether or not admission is charged.

No one shall make any changes in this title for the purpose of production. No part of this book may be reproduced, stored in a retrieval system, or transmitted in any form, by any means, now known or yet to be invented, including mechanical, electronic, photocopying, recording, videotaping, or otherwise, without the prior written permission of the publisher. No one shall upload this title, or part of this title, to any social media websites.

The right of Steve Brown, Justin Greene, Vivian Nicholson and Stephen Smith to be identified as author of this work has been asserted in accordance with Section 77 of the Copyright, Designs and Patents Act 1988.

SPEND SPEND SPEND

First performed at the West Yorkshire Playhouse, May 1998, with the following cast:

Viv	Rosemary Ashe
Young Viv	Sophie-Louise Dann
The Bank Manager	Jonathan D. Ellis
Mrs Waterman	Michelle Fine
Beautician/ Air Hostess	Melissa Jacques
Johnny Love	Andrew Kennedy
George	Neil McCaul
Keith	Nigel Richards
The Solicitor/Matt	Paul Thornley
Sue	Sara Williams
Company	

Boys: Veron Bush, Sam Dunn, Andrew Foxcroft, Christopher Symonds **Girls**: Katrina Brown, Carly Klineberg, Siobhan Mullins, Katie Thorntan **Men**: Anthony James Brown, Roy Clarke, Dan Laythorpe, Paul Simons, Michael Willis **Women**: Val Duggan, Maureen Harrison, Melanie Klineberg, Janet Sherwin, Joanna Wardman

Directed by Justin Greene
Designed by Nicki Turner
Musical staging and choreography by Pat Garrett
Musical Director and Arranger: Dane Preece
Lighting designed by Robert Bryan
Sound by Mic Pool

The musical was subsequently presented in the West

End of London at the Piccadilly Theatre on October 12th 1999 in a revised version, with the following cast:

Salon Customer/Miner's Wife/Garforth Resident Lorraine Chappell
Viv Barbara Dickson
Miner's Wife/Florrie/Grieving Relative Susan Fay
Salon Customer/Bridesmaid/Stewardess Jane Fowler
Keith Steve Houghton
Mrs Waterman/MC/Landlady Marjorie Keys
Young Viv/Sue Rachel Leskovac
Road Sweeper/Pools Man/Husband 4 Craig Nicholls
Vicar/Bank Manager/Husband 5 Stuart Nurse
Business Man/Estate Agent/Husband 3 Stuart Pendred
Cinema Manager/Bruce Forsyth/Policeman Robin Samson
George Jeff Shankley
Viv's Mother/Salon Manageress Nicola Sloane
Miner, Doorman/Taxman Duncan Smith
Fireman Dancer/Miner/Stranger Jamie Somers
Bridesmaid/ Single Mother/Daughter Mary Stockley
Matt/Fraudulent Granny/Son Paul Thornley
Child/Viv's son Alexander Pepe, Liam O'Bryne, Andrew Stylianou
Child/Viv's daughter Alana Asher, Sophie Wallis, Bethanie Snell
Swing Gary Milner
Swing Rebecca Barnes

Directed by Jeremy Sams
Designed by Lez Brotherston
Lighting by Mark Henderson
Sound by Rick Clarke
Choreographed by Craig Horwood
Musical Director; Dane Preece

Only this revised version is published in an Acting Edition and is the only version available for amateur production.

CHARACTERS

Viv
Mrs Waterman
Sue, Viv's granddaughter
Young Viv, Viv's younger self
George, Viv's dad
Matt, Viv's first husband
Viv's **Mother**
Keith, Viv's second husband
Estate Agent
Bank Manager
Policeman
Florrie, housekeeper
Tax Man
Viv's **Daughter**
Viv's **Son**

Other parts played by members of the company: Customers, Beautician, Saturday girl, Receptionist, 2 love-sick lads, Cinema Manager, Miners, Miners' Wives, Vicar, Bridesmaids, Photographers, Church Choir, Reporters, Tiller Girls, Bruce Forsyth, Woman, Man, Drinker, Granny/fraudster, Pools Man, Pub Landlady, Jealous Woman, Stranger, Neighbours, Stewardess, Hotel Doorman, Mourners, Tart, Keith's Mum and Dad, Keith's Grandad, Husbands 3, 4 & 5, Judge, Council Man and Bailiffs

MUSICAL NUMBERS

Act I

	Piccadilly Overture (Part 1)	Orchestral
	One in a Million (Part 2)	Viv, Female Chorus
No. 1	Salon Mystique	Viv, Mrs Waterman, Sue
No. 2	Ice-cream Girl	Matt, Love-sick Lads, Viv
No. 3	I'll Take Care of Thee	George, Miners, Viv, Mother
No. 4	Upstairs in My Room	George, Mother, Viv, Young Viv
No. 5	Sexual Happening	Viv, Young Viv, Matt
No. 6	Special Day	Young Viv, Viv, Church Choir, George, Company
No. 7	The Boy Next Door	Young Viv, Keith, Viv
No. 8	The Scars of Love	Viv, Young Viv, Keith, Chorus
No. 9	John Collier	George, Mother, Young Viv, Keith, Chorus
No. 10	The Win	Viv, Young Viv, Keith, Chorus
No. 11	Two Rooms	George, Keith, Young Viv, Viv
No. 12	Spend Spend Spend	Viv, Keith, Young Viv, Bruce, Chorus

Act II

No. 13	The Miners' Arms	Viv, Keith, Pools Man, Young Viv, Chorus
No. 13a	Take Me Away	Young Viv, Keith, Viv
No. 14	Garforth	Estate Agent, Young Viv, Keith, Viv, Chorus
No. 14a	Garforth Coda	Keith, Bank Manager, Viv, Chorus
No. 14b	Take Me Away	Viv, Stewardess, Young Viv, Keith, Doorman
No. 15	Drinking in America	Young Viv, Viv
No. 16	Canary in a Cage	Keith
No. 17	Canary (Part 2)	Keith, Viv, Policeman
No. 18	Who's Gonna Love Me	Young Viv, Viv
No. 19	Dance of the Suits	Bank Manager, Tax Man
No. 19a	Pieces of Me	Viv, George, Mother, Chorus, Council Man
No. 20	A Brand New Husband	Young Viv, Husbands, George, Viv
No. 21	Spent	

Chorus, Viv, Young Viv, Bailiffs

No. 22	Canary in a Cage (Reprise)	Young Viv, Viv
No. 23	Mother, Oh, Mother	Young Viv, Viv, Stranger, Daughter, Son
No. 24	Roll Back the Years (Reprise)	Viv, Mrs Waterman
No. 25	Instrumental	
No. 26	Instrumental	
No. 27	Spend Spend Spend (Reprise)	Company

Score and band parts are available on hire from Samuel French Ltd

ACT I
Piccadilly Overture (Part 1)
Scene 1

Salon Mystique — a beauty salon. Yorkshire

The Lights come up and the music continues to underscore

There are customers including Mrs Waterman, a beautician, a Saturday girl, and a Receptionist. Mrs Waterman holds a glossy magazine

On another part of the stage, Viv stands out of the scene

Viv (*to the audience*) I know what you're thinking. What's it like having everything? Well, you still want something.

One in a Million (Part 2)

Company (*singing*)   I want it. I want it.

Viv (*speaking*) There's always something.

Company (*singing*) I'm absolutely desp'rate.
                I want it, I want it.
                And when at last I get it — —
                Me problems are over — —
                If only.
Customers   I want that dress
                If it were twenty quid less.
                I want them bathroom fittings.
                Ooh, I want that cake.
Receptionist   I want a loan
                To buy a shop of me own.
                I want to start an empire.
Beautician   I wanna break
Company   I want it.
                Them curtains.
                That camera.
                A brand new Vauxhall Astra.
                This telly.
                That handbag.
                A mini-disc and then I'd be happy.
                If only, if only.

Saturday Girl	I want a man.
Customers	I want a fabulous tan.
Beautician	I want a week in Malta, for me holidays.
Customers	A diamond ring.
Receptionist	Designer everything.
Customer	I want a fitted kitchen.
Saturday Girl	I want a raise.

Viv moves into the scene of Salon Mystique

Company Hey look!
It's her what won the Pools!
She must have had a million quid.
And tossed it all against the wall.
By God, by God, it makes you sick.
To think of how she wasted it!

Viv (*to the audience*) As you can see, I'm still known and loved in my part of the world. All that money. She'll never have to work again.
Receptionist (*to Mrs Waterman*) Good-afternoon, madam.
Mrs Waterman I've an appointment with the Pools lady.
Viv (*to Mrs Waterman*) Hallo, love.
Mrs Waterman Waterman's the name, Mrs Waterman.

No. 1 Salon Mystique

Viv (*singing*) At Salon Mystique
To tell you the truth
We haven't the secret of eternal youth.
But here are the creams
The powder and oils
We slap on your skin an' 'air
To make you feel like flippin' royals.
Your spirits are down
We'll give them a lift
We've not seen the laughter line
We couldn't shift.
We're fighting your flab
It soon disappears.
We'll turn back the clock
We'll roll back the years.
We have the know how
With an oil of avocado.
Soon we will show how
You can look like Brigitte Bardot.

Act I, Scene 1   3

Viv
Receptionist } The young Brigitte Bardot.

Viv (*speaking*) What can we do for you today?

Mrs Waterman (*singing*) I wanna new look.
Viv We will transform you madam — in a trice!
Mrs Waterman Well, summat like 'er.

Mrs Waterman holds up a photograph of Michelle Pfeiffer on the front of her magazine

Viv What? Michelle Pfeiffer? Why not; very nice!
Mrs Waterman Or Claudia Schiffer — which do you prefer?
Viv Be less ambitious, love. That's my advice.
Mrs Waterman So how did it feel?
Viv Hey up! I think I know what's coming now!
Mrs Waterman You being so rich!
Viv Then blowin' every cent, you soppy cow!
Mrs Waterman Then chucking it all away
(And now she's broke, the silly bitch!)
I bet you feel daft.
Viv Oh yes, Ms Pfeiffer, don't you like to gloat.
Mrs Waterman You must have been thick.
Viv Pass me that towel — I'll shove it down her throat.
Mrs Waterman Just thinking of all the waste — it makes you sick.
Viv Who did your hair last?
He'd had a few beers
Sit back in your seat
And roll back the years.

Roll back the years,
Old dears.
Fight the good fight,
Wrinklies must unite.
Roll back the years.

Mrs Waterman (*speaking*) So how did it feel like when you won all that money?

Sue runs in

Sue Hey, Gran!

Viv Sue!

Sue (*singing*) Hey Gran! Guess what I've done?
I've only gone and won it.
Viv (*speaking*) What have you won?
Sue (*singing*) I've only won the Lottery.
Waterman (*speaking*) You Nicholsons are jammy bleeders!
Sue (*singing*) Guess what?
I'm gonna blow the lot!
I'm gonna be like you, Gran!
I'm gonna Spend! Spend! Spend!
  (*Speaking*) Twenty-five quid!

Viv That's what it felt like! At least, I think that's what it felt like...

The Lights change

  All the Company exit, apart from Viv

Viv continues with the song as the scene changes

Scene 2

Castleford Street

No. 1 Salon Mystique (continued)

Viv (*singing*) Roll back the years, the years
Picture the past,
Time that went so fast
Roll back the years,
All the things you can't forget,
Funny memories and yet,
Somehow they're beautiful.

  Young Viv enters

Roll back the years
The years.
Try to recall ...

  George, Viv's dad, enters

Viv stands apart from the scene as a narrator for her memories, and remains on stage throughout the rest of the Act

Act I, Scene 3

George (*speaking*) Viv, lass! Lend your dad a couple of bob!
Viv (*singing*)   Was it real at all?
Young Viv (*speaking*) Later, Dad, when I get paid!
Viv (*singing*)   Roll back the years,
George (*speaking*) Hey! What's all that muck on your face? (*He moves to wipe the muck off Young Viv's face*)
Viv (*singing*)   See the girl I used to be.
Young Viv (*speaking*) Get off! I'm late as it is.
George (*speaking*) Hey! Viv!
Viv (*singing*)   Always late — aye, that were me.
George (*speaking*) Don't tha bring no trouble home.
Viv (*singing*)   And maybe — beautiful ...?

Young Viv exits

The Lights change

George exits

Scene 3

The Cinema

A neon sign lights up. There are pictures of Fifties film stars

Three love-sick lads, including Matt, are waiting to have their tickets torn. They sing

No. 2 Ice-cream Girl

Lads   Where is our dream girl?
                Where is our dream girl?
                Where is our dream girl?

A furious cinema manager enters, wearing an ice-cream tray

Manager   Bloody ice-cream girl!

Lads   Where is our dream girl
          Pure as vanilla in a cone
          She stands alone
          I stand in line

Pretty ice-cream girl
Pepsi could never taste as sweet
Please choose the seat
Right next to mine

Heaven knows how much
I worship and adore her
Lord above, I'd gladly implore her to
Give me a — Kia-ora

Young Viv enters

The music continues

(*Speaking*) Viv, you're late!
Young Viv Sorry, Mr Balcombe. (*She puts on the ice-cream tray*)

The cinema manager exits

Lads (*singing*) Ev'rybody knows,
The ice-cream girl.
Everybody wants,
The ice-cream girl, so young, so fine and fair.
Diana Dors cannot compare.
Ev'rybody loves,
The ice-cream girl.

You are my dream girl,
Soon as the intermission starts,
You melt our hearts.
You are the star,
Pretty ice-cream girl,
Nobody's looking at the flick,
Dish on a stick,
That's what you are,
It's not your torchlight,
That dazzles — but your beauty.
Viv All the lads were after one thing,
And I don't mean tutti-frutti.
Lads Ev'rybody knows,
The ice-cream girl.
Ev'rybody wants,
The ice-cream girl.
So coy, so cool and curved,
We've got the back row seat reserved.

Act I, Scene 3

> Ev'rybody loves,
> The ice-cream girl.
>
> Ev'rybody knows,
> The ice-cream girl.
> Ev'rybody wants,
> The ice-cream girl.
> A fountain still untapped,
> A choc-ice yet to be unwrapped.

Young Viv (*speaking*) Hey! You'll get slapped.

Lads (*singing*) Ev'rybody loves,
> The ice-cream girl.

Two of the lads, not including Matt, each give a letter to Young Viv and move towards the exit as they sing

> You are my dream girl.
> You are my dream girl.

The two lads exit

Matt You are my dream girl.

Matt takes the ice-cream tray

The music continues to underscore

(*Speaking*) I'll take this.
Viv Them lads were always giving me letters. I had a right collection.
Young Viv (*reading the letters*) What's an 'ard on?
Viv I hadn't a clue what he meant. Truly — I were that green.
Matt Can I walk you home?
Viv I were waiting for Mr Right.
Matt I'll buy you a bag of chips
Viv Well, you can't wait forever!
Young Viv All right, Matt!
Viv And you don't want to walk home on your own. Not at closing time — not in Castleford!

Young Viv and Matt exit

The Lights change

SCENE 4

Outisde the Miners' Arms *pub*

A group of drunken Miners are propelled onto the street from the Miners' Arms. *The group includes George. They sing*

No 3. I'll Take Care of Thee

George ⎱ Yorkshiremen are England's finest
Miners ⎰ England's finest that is clear.
　　　　　　Yorkshiremen are strong and decent
　　　　　　Yorkshiremen can take their beer.
　　　　　　Yes, we can take our beer
　　　　　　We'll take care of thee.
　　　　　　We'll take care of thee.

Young Viv and Matt enter

The music continues

Young Viv (*speaking*) Eck, it's me dad.
Matt Shall I introduce meself?
Young Viv Don't be so daft, Matt, just bugger off quick.
George Viv, lass! Who's that with you? Is it — a lad?!
Young Viv (*to Matt*) Bugger off!
George How many times must I tell you?

(*Singing*)　　Yorkshire lads are mucky bastards
　　　　　　Dirty, mucky bastards all.
　　　　　　Keep your hand upon your ha'penny
　　　　　　Else you're riding for a fall.
　　　　　　You're riding for a fall
　　　　　　I'll take care of thee
　　　　　　I'll take care of thee.
　　　　　　I'm strong as an ox
　　　　　　I'm tough as old boots
　　　　　　I'm fitter than any lad.
　　　　　　They're not worth a light
　　　　　　There's not one around
　　　　　　Who'll love you like your dad.
　　　　　　I'll take care of thee.

(*Speaking*) D'you know my daughter, boys? Isn't she a beauty?

Act I, Scene 4

Miners (*singing*) Castleford girls
There's none that are finer.
Castleford girls
A sight to behold.
Castleford girls
Look after their fathers.
You're never lonely when you're old
With Castleford girls around.
Viv The summers were longer.
The beer tasted stronger.
Those Castleford nights
Could get quite continental,
When we danced the conga.

Women, including Viv's mother, enter. They join the miners

In Viv's memory, the street is now teeming with life

All Laughing, talking, dancing in the streets,
Sing songs, ding-dongs, dominoes and darts.
Front doors open wide like people's hearts.
Viv No video
No satellite
To keep you glued
To telly all night.
Quite happy though
We lived on tick
Or is the mem'ry
Playing a trick — on me?
The roads weren't congested,
The yobs got arrested.
Your children could go out and play in the street
Without being molested.
All Castleford folk
Look after each other.
Castleford folk
Look after their own.
Castleford folk
Are just like a fam'ly.
You'll never have to be alone
With Castleford folk around.

The Chorus move into a funeral procession. The men carry a coffin

Viv	I remember the time when Billy Barstow died
Killed down the mine
And ev'rybody cried.
Young apprentice he was
Weren't no more than a lad
We all had a whip round for his mum and dad.
United in sorrow as we were in joy
And ev'ry mother thought — —
Viv
Mother	That could be my own boy.
Viv	Oh Billy, poor Billy
Who'll take care of thee.
Who'll take care of thee now tha's gone.
George
Miners	Yorkshiremen can tell a story
Tales to make you laugh or cry.
Yorkshiremen cannot be beaten
Lancashire, we'll black your eye.
Yorkshiremen will stay in Yorkshire
Yorkie boys until we die.
George	I'll take care of thee
I'll take care of thee.
I'm solid as rock
A tower of strength.
Mother	You're drunk as a lord
You're thick as two planks.
And I'll take care of thee …

(*Speaking*) Tha' bugger!

The miners lift George up on to their shoulders

All	Yorkshiremen are England's finest
England's finest, that is clear.
Yorkshiremen are strong and decent
Yorkshiremen can take their beer.
Yes, we can take our beer
We'll take care of thee
We'll take care of thee!

The women exit. Viv's mother, Young Viv and Viv remain

Miner Hey! Missis! We've got George here. Shall we carry him upstairs for thee?

Viv Mam says — —

Act I, Scene 4   11

Mother No. I don't want to put you to any trouble lads. Leave him int' yard!

The miners, with George, exit

Viv They had some right set-tos, me mam and dad, so I hid upstairs in my room, but I still got caught in the middle.

There is a lighting change

No. 4 Upstairs in My Room

George (*off stage; singing*) Daughter, oh, daughter
Come and open the door
Where is your heart and compassion?
Mother Leave him down there, love.
Now his beer money's gone
He wants the food what's on ration.
George (*off stage*) Chuck us me ration book
So's least I can eat.
Viv There's a black market man
Who lives down our street
Father goes to him and he flogs off our grub
George (*off stage*) Lend us a shilling
For an hour down the pub.

Mother	**George** (*off stage*)
Leave him, dear daughter of mine	Hurry, dear daughter of mine
Leave him, dear daughter of mine	Hurry, dear daughter of mine
Leave him, dear daughter of mine	Hurry, dear daughter of mine

Viv   Me dad's epileptic,
Me mother is ill.

Mother (*speaking; to George*) You make me sick!

Viv (*singing*)   She knows she should leave him
But she never will do.

George (*speaking; off stage*) Liz! Open up, love.

Viv (*singing*)   Me mum is a martyr
Me dad's a non-starter
The family's future is gloomy.

George (*speaking; off stage*) Sod this!

Young Viv	(*singing*) I'm better off hiding,
	Upstairs in me room.
Viv	Me dad never works
	Spends his life on the sick.
Mother	Daughter, oh, daughter
	While your father's asleep.
Viv	Don't leave nothin' lyin'
	Around or he'll nick it.
Mother	Let's hide the tea and the sugar
Viv	A boozer? The worst
	He is constantly thirsty
	But here there's no harm can come to me — —
Mother	Under the mattress
	Now and hush! Not a word.
Young Viv	Not while I can daydream
	Upstairs in me room.
Mother	He'll never look there the bugger!

Viv's mother exits and George enters

George   Daughter, oh, daughter
I'm not long for this world
I feel the end slowly nearin'.
Daughter, I ask you
Lend us ten bleedin' bob
So I may leave with some beer in!

Where has thy mother
Hid the sugar and tea?
Find it and flog it,
Then bring brass back to me.

Don't tha' say nowt lass
Or else tha'll get some fist
Hurry dear daughter of mine.

George exits

Young Viv   I'd look through me letters
Them lads on me mind.
Could anyone love me
Be gentle and kind too.

Act I, Scene 4

      I'd start fantasizing
      And hey it's surprising.
      The funniest shivers run through me
      I hope no-one finds me
      Upstairs in me room.

George enters

George   Daughter, oh, daughter
      What's this under tha' bed!
      Summat that tha' wants kept hidden?
      Who wrote these letters?
      Is tha' seeing some lad?
      Have I not said, that's forbidden?
      He touched your thingies?
      Tha's a bag and a whore
      Filth, muck and rubbish!
      Tha' won't see him no more.

George beats Young Viv

      How could you shame me?
      I'll take care of thee!
      Now tha's gettin' what for
      Thou art no daughter of mine!

George exits

Young Viv I know me dad loves me
      He knocks me about.
      He says I been dirty
      Although I've done nowt — yet!
      If that's what you bleedin'
      Well get just for readin'
      I might as well let someone do me.

Matt enters

      Hey, Matt!
      Tha's got lucky.
      Upstairs in me room.

Young Viv and Matt begin to make love

The lighting changes

  Matt exits

SCENE 5

Viv and Young Viv are on stage

No. 5 Sexual Happening

Viv (*singing*)   Some folk like to call it friggin'
Fornicatin', jig-a-jiggin'
Hide the sausage, slap and tickle or a lay.
Shaftin', shaggin', screwin', humpin'
Rumpy-pumpy, pumpy-pumpin'
Bangin', bonkin', rogerin' your end away.
But I call it
A beautiful mem'ry
The deed of joy
A sexual happening.
Bodies touching, got no clothes on
That nice tingle, skin together
No more kids' stuff, it's the real thing.

Young Viv   Now the world looks very different
It's a place of sexual happenings
Just waiting out there for me

  A Businessman enters

I can cha-cha, I can rhumba
Now at last I've got your number
'Cos I'm thinking just the same as you.
Doing the dance of love
Once I felt like Cinderella
Now I'd polka any fella.
Any fella that I bump into
Doing the dance of love.

Doing the dance
Doing the dance

Act I, Scene 5   15

>   Doing the
>   Doing it
>   Doing
>   Doing the dance ev'rybody does.
>   Doin' the dance
>   Doing the dance
>   Doing the
>   Doing it
>   Doing
>   Doin' the dance, the dance of love!

The Businessman exits as a Road Sweeper enters

>   There's a million men in Leeds
>   And some are flowers, some are weeds
>   But the whole damn blooming shipment
>   Has the necess'ry equipment
>   That can satisfy my needs.
>
>   Wanna tell the whole damn street
>   Now that I've lost it, I'm complete,
>   I don't know about the tango
>   But it sure takes two to bang-o!
>   Come and dance me off
>   Me feet.
>
>   I'm doing the dance
>   Doing the dance
>   Doing the
>   Doing it
>   Doing
>   Doing the dance everybody does.
>   Doing the dance
>   Doing the dance
>   Doing the
>   Doing it
>   Doing
>   Doin' the dance, the dance of love!

The Road Sweeper exits as a Fireman enters

Young Viv   Good-day complete total stranger
                What would you be like in bed?
                What would you look like

Stark bollock naked?
These are the questions that pop in my head.
D'you know, complete total stranger
I watched you when you walked by,
I like a nice bottom
And fellers that's got 'em
And you qualify
Complete total stranger.

Doing the dance
Doing the dance
Doing the
Doing it
Doing
Doing the dance everybody does.
Doing the dance
Doing the dance
Doing the
Doing it
Doing
Doin' the dance
Doing it
Doing
Doin' the dance
Doing it
Doing
Doin' the dance
The dance of love.

The Fireman exits as Matt enters

Young Viv returns to Matt

Some folk like to call it friggin'
Fornicatin', jig-a-jiggin'
Hide the sausage, slap and tickle or a lay.
Shaftin', shaggin', screwin', humpin'
Rumpy-pumpy, pumpy-pumpin'
Bangin', bonkin', rogerin' your end away.
But I call it
A beautiful mem'ry
The deed of joy
A sexual happening.

Viv   Second time were disappointing

Act I, Scene 6   17

	Not exciting, like the first time
	His report reads "must try harder"
Young Viv	Where's the romance?
Matt	That were nice love.
Young Viv	There'll be other sexual happenings
	But I won't be seeing him again.

The music continues to underscore and segues into **No. 6**

The Lights change

   Young Viv and Matt exit

Viv (*speaking*) Famous last words! Sweet sixteen and four months gone!

SCENE 6

Viv's Wedding Day

The company gather as a wedding day congregation. Included in the congregation is George, Viv's dad; Viv's mum, a photographer and bridesmaids. There is a church choir and a Vicar. Matt and Young Viv stand at the front of the congregation

No. 6 Special Day

Vicar (*singing*)	We gather in the sight of God
	To join together Matt and Viv
	In wedlock so that they may be — —
Chorus	Pissed off and bored and
	At each other's throats.
Vicar	As long as they both shall live
Chorus	This is a special day
	A day of song and celebration.
Bridesmaids	One ev'ry young girl dreams
	Of having, it's her special day.
Chorus	This is a dream come true.
Young Viv	Please someone, wake me up and save me.
Chorus	Beautiful flowers ev'rywhere
Young Viv	Like flowers for my grave.
Vicar	Exchange the rings and take thy vows
	To love, to honour and obey.
Photographer	Her father looks quite overcome,

Church Choir	Been on the beer he's absolutely sloshed!
Chorus	On oh, such a special day.
George	This is a special day
	I hope tha'll not live to regret it.
	Tha' can still pull out now
	It's not too late to pull out yet.

(*To Matt; speaking*) And tha should've pulled out quicker!
(*Singing, to Young Viv*) Don't leave thy father dear
You're far too young to be a wife lass.

Young Viv	Somebody stop me, I'm about
	To throw away my life.
Vicar	Speak up now lass and say thy part
	Remember, God looks down on you
	Don't make your husband wait all day
	I've got another wedding in an hour
	Repeat after me "I do".
Chorus	I do.
Young Viv	Make a promise that you'll never have my heart.
Chrous	I do.
Young Viv	Swear to God that I'll pretend and play the part.
Chorus	I do.
Young Viv	Undertake to search for happiness one day.
Chorus	I do.
Young Viv	Still believe that better times aren't far away.
Chours	I do.
Young Viv	Keep the hope that out there somewhere life is true.
Chorus	I do.
Young Viv	Want somebody, though it never will be you.

The entire congregation exits, leaving Viv and Young Viv

Viv	This is a special day,
	You bid farewell to fun and freedom.
	Ta'ra to fantasy,
	Goodbye the girl you used to be.

Viv hands Young Viv a dustpan and brush

	Fall down upon your knees,
	Wait hand and foot upon your husband.
	Cook, clean and stay at home,
	Like ev'ry good wife does.
Young Viv	There must be more to life than this,

Act I, Scene 7   19

                  This bloody awful marital bliss.

Keith enters, carrying a canoe over his shoulder

Viv   Then I saw him.
Young Viv   Then I saw him.
Viv   Mr Right appeared before too long
                  Making up for everything that's — —
Young Viv   Wrong in my life, just by existing
                  Now I can sing a different song
                  Who cares if he's rich or poor
                  The boy next door ...

Keith (*speaking*) Hallo, love.

Lighting change

The music continues and segues into **Song No. 7**

SCENE 7

The same; immediately following

No.7 The Boy Next Door

Young Viv (*singing*)   Oh, the boy next door
                            Could he be the answer to my prayer?
                            Looked across the wall,
                            Looked across the wall and he were there.
                            Tall and handsome, now I'm goggle-eyed,
                            Long to tell him what I feel inside.

  (*Speaking; of the canoe*) Oi, Hiawatha! What do you think this is? Cowes week? Get that shifted.
Keith I was just gonna keep it out here for a while. It's all right, isn't it?
Young Viv No it bloody isn't. It's sticking on to my property.
Keith It's a bloody fence — —
Young Viv Now listen, moosh. Owt of yours touches owt of mine, there'll be hell to pay, all right!?

  (*Singing*)   Oh, the boy next door
                    What about the way he looked at me?
                    Well, he fancies me, it's plain to see.

　　　　　　　　　Wooh!
　　　　　　　　　Oh, the boy next door.

　　Young Viv exits

Keith　　　　Oh, the girl next door
　　　　　　　　　Suddenly, my heart begins to ache.
　　　　　　　　　She's the one for me
　　　　　　　　　She's the one for me and no mistake.
　　　　　　　　　Flowers blooming now that she is near
　　　　　　　　　Will she whisper what I long to hear.

Young Viv enters wearing a bra and skirt

Young Viv (*speaking*) Didn't you hear me the first bleedin' time? Get that thing moved. Get it cowin' moved. Or I'll get Council to have it scrapped. What you gawping at?
Keith Nowt, Mrs Davies. Nice earrings.

Young Viv exits

　　(*Singing*)　　Oh, the girl next door
　　　　　　　　　Tiny Angel fallen from the sky.
　　　　　　　　　Young and beautiful and kinda shy.
　　　　　　　　　Wooh
　　　　　　　　　Oh, the girl next door.
Viv　　　　　It must be love
　　　　　　　　　You waited and waited.
　　　　　　　　　It must be love
　　　　　　　　　You're getting frustrated.
　　　　　　　　　He lives with his gran,
　　　　　　　　　You live with a man,
　　　　　　　　　It's too complicated,
　　　　　　　　　It must be love.

　　　　　　　　　It must be love
　　　　　　　　　Your feelings are hidden.
　　　　　　　　　It must be love
　　　　　　　　　The fruit is forbidden.
　　　　　　　　　You're already wed,
　　　　　　　　　The trouble ahead,
　　　　　　　　　Can't be overridden,
　　　　　　　　　It must be love.

　　　　　　　　　Oh, the girl next door

Act I, Scene 8

>Married with a kid, she's quite a catch.
>Oh, the boy next door
>Likes to pick his teeth clean with a match.
>Storms are brewing and they're bound to come
>Cupid's arrows sticking in yer bum.

Matt and Young Viv enter. Young Viv is now dressed

Keith (*speaking*) 'ow do.
Matt Chippy were closed.
Young Viv Oh, piss off! Hey, while you're here, take our Steven round me Mam's.
Matt Why, where you going, love?
Young Viv "Where you going, love." Out! Now piss off!

Matt exits

Viv (*singing*) Oh, the boy next door.
No, it's not the stuff of true romance,
If they stuck a padlock on his pants,
Couldn't make it no harder to score
With the boy next door.
Oh, the boy next door.
Keith (*speaking*) Oh, the girl next door.
Young Viv Oh, the girl next door.
Keith Oh, the girl next door.

Lighting change

>*Keith exits*

SCENE 8

A Dance Hall

The Company enters as dancers at the hall

Young Viv remains on stage

No. 8 The Scars of Love

Viv (*speaking*) Some things are just meant to happen, aren't they? You can't avoid them. And some things stay with you forever — and some people.
Keith enters

Like you — you handsome bastard. You've always stayed here. (*She puts hand to heart*)

(*Singing*)
    I won't forget
    After the dance,
    Fin'lly at last
    Here was a chance,
    We make the first
    Prints in the snow,
    You take my hand
    That's when I know.

Viv watches her younger self and Keith as they dance

    Start with a touch
    Then with a kiss,
    Nothing could be
    Better than this,
    Better than some
    Movie romance,
    I won't forget
    After the dance.

    But though the scars of love
    Always remain,
    They're worth the pain of it
    Love that tears the soul,
    And breaks the heart
    Is all a part of it.

    You wipe away your tears
    But one thing never disappears,
    The wound that time won't heal
    That no one sees but you
    Will always feel,
    And so it hurts, but all is fair
    We all must bear,
    The scars of …

Young Viv and Keith stop dancing. They hold hands and move away from the other dancers as if to leave the dance hall. The other dancers stop dancing

During the following, the lighting changes and the couple are outside in the night air

Viv   You stay here,

Act I, Scene 8

Young Viv	Now it is real.
Viv	Dreams of you never go away,
Keith	Now we begin,
Viv	You are with me ev'ryday.
Young Viv	Lips upon lips …
Viv	Ev'ry night
	I see you appear.
Keith	Skin upon skin …
Viv	Crystal clear
	In my mind's eye.
Young Viv ⎫	We are complete …
Keith ⎭	
Viv	Not one mem'ry
	Will ever die.
Young Viv ⎫	We become whole ...
Keith ⎭	
Viv	Love holds on
	When the flesh has gone.
Young Viv	Joined in the blood …
Viv	After ev'rything
	You stay here.
Young Viv ⎫	Joined at the soul …
Keith ⎭	
Chorus	And tho', the scars of love
	Always remain,
	They're worth the pain of it,
	Love that tears the soul
	And breaks the heart,
	Is all a part of it.
Viv	You wipe away your tears
	But one things that never disappears,
	The wounds that time won't heal
	That no-one sees, but you
	Will always feel.
	And so it hurts, but all is fair
	We all must bear
	The scars of love.

Chorus sing on an "ah"

The music continues to underscore

Keith It'd freeze the balls off a pawnbrokers!

Matt enters

The dancers exit slowly during the following

Matt Get inside. Keep away from her.
Keith No. You keep away. I've been with her now, I love her, and I don't want you nor nobody else touching her ever again.
Matt You won't stay with me then?
Young Viv Not if you had a million pound!

Viv (*singing*) You wipe away your tears
But one thing never disappears,
The wounds that time won't heal
That no-one sees,
But you will always feel
And so it hurts,
But all is fair
We all must bear,
The scars of love.

Music (**No 8a**) *continues to underscore*

Viv So, I divorced Matt and married Keith. We should have lived happily ever after, except I was still married to John Collier. Keith was a miner an' all. They were all John Collier round our way. They had no choice. Either you went down pit or you went on assistance. It were tradition. Like our wedding reception. Pie and ale in't *Miners' Arms*.

The Lighting changes

The Company enter as Miners and Miners' Wives; including George and Viv's mum. They bring on pints of ale

No. 9 John Collier

George A toast! To John Collier!

(*Singing*) John Collier's life is harder than any
The few supplying coal for the many,
He risks his life for barely a penny
Pity poor John Collier,
Pity poor John Collier.
Miners John Collier's life is tough, no mistaking

Act I, Scene 8

	He shovels coal, his poor back is breaking,
	All for the pittance he'll be a-making
	Pity poor John Collier,
	Pity poor John Collier.
	So toll the bell
	And know him well,
	He must return to the pit of hell.
	The devil waits,
	At Hades' gates
	And there he'll burn — John Collier.
Mother	Cobblers! I'll tell thee what's what!
	John Collier's wife deserves all the pity
	She makes ends meet with nowt in the kitty,
	The pay is crap, the hours are shitty.
	Pity poor John Collier? No!
	Pity Mrs Collier.
Young Viv	John Collier's life is skivin' or snoozin'
Young Viv ⎫	Or down the Miners' Arms he'll go boozin'
Wives ⎭	Or playing cards — and sure to be losin'.
	Pity poor John Collier!
	Pity poor John Collier!
Wives	So toe the line
	You lazy swine,
	There's work to do and it's down the mine.
	Now take your pick
	And make it quick,
	Good riddance to — —
Miners	John Collier's life, not one of us chose it,
	It's dang'rous, dirty, all of us knows it.
	We hate the pit but don't wanna close it,
	Pity poor John Collier
	Pity poor John Collier.

Young Viv and Keith move away from the action

	But we never complain
	No we never complain,
	Never moan or groan or grumble.
Miners ⎫	
Wives ⎭	Never complain

No we never complain,
Well, it wouldn't do any good.

The Lighting fades slowly on the Miners and their Wives, and focuses on Keith and Young Viv

Keith   Oh, Lord above
We did make love,
Three times already, don't push and shove.
You always keep
Me from me sleep,
Till I'm half dead — John Collier.
Young Viv   Just once more Keith
Use this last sheath,
With me on top and you underneath.
Keith   I won't be fit
To work at pit
But that won't stop — John Collier.
Wives   John Collier thinks he's our Lord and master
Paul Getty never spent money faster,
A walking, talking, mining disaster
Pity Mrs Collier,
Pity Mrs Collier.
All   John Collier's life is harder than any
The few supplying coal for the many
He risks his life for barely a penny
Pity poor John Collier
Pity poor John Collier
Pity poor John Collier
Pity poor John Collier.

The Miners and their Wives exit

Young Viv and Keith remain on stage

Scene 9

Viv's and Keith's home

The Lights come up fully

Viv Hard times? Soon we had two kids to feed, then three kids, then four. All on a miner's pay. Strike pay an' all. Hard times?

Act I, Scene 9

Young Viv Gas bill.
Viv We dreaded the rent man calling.

There is a pounding on the front door

Young Viv Who's that?

No. 10 The Win

Viv The wolf,
The wolf were at the door.
You'd better shut the window,
And quick before love does a bunk.

Keith (*speaking*) Who's at door love?
Young Viv No-one.

Viv (*singing*) Only two quid
Left to us name,
Week in week out
Always the same.
Begging for crumbs
So it goes on,
Even the mice
Packed up and gone.
Young Viv Does tha' know …
Keith What is it love?
Young Viv What I think we should
Do with this.
Keith What have I missed?
Young Viv Last two quid, let's
Blow it in.
Keith What does tha' mean?
Young Viv Blow it all at the
Pub tonight.
Keith Go and get pissed?
Young Viv And to hell with,
All of 'em.
Keith That's the idea!
Young Viv Get me dad round to
Watch the kids.
Keith That's me lass, Viv!
Young Viv Life just isn't worth livin' if
You're forever afraid of it.

Young Viv ⎫ That's not your way,
Keith ⎭ No way to live.

The music continues to underscore and Young Viv and Keith dance around the room. They start getting ready for a night out. Young Viv changes and Keith shaves

Keith Put the radio on love. Time for Pools.

Viv turns on the radio

Chorus (*off stage; singing*) Arsenal, one — Birmingham City, one.
Keith   A draw!
                Hey love — I got a draw.
Young Viv   Oh aye?
                That's nice.
Chorus   Chelsea, one — Blackburn Rovers, one.
                Wolverhampton Wanderers, one — Cardiff City, one.
Keith   That's two!
                Hey cock, I've got two more now.
Viv   Does tha' know
                What I think we should
                Do with this
                Last two quid?
                Let's blow it in
                Blow it all
                At the pub.
Chorus   Swansea Town, three — Middlesborough, three.
Keith   That's four,
                That's four and that's for sure.
                Now all I need is four more.
Young Viv   Tha's asking for a miracle
Chorus   Halifax, one — Port Vale, one.
Viv   Roll back the years
                My dears,
                Don't stray so far,
                Stay the way you are.
Chorus   Darlington, three — Bradford City, three.
                Oldham Athletic, nil — Stockport County, nil
Keith   That's it!
                That's it! That's seven now
                That's seven! Where's me trousers?
Young Viv   Well, at a guess, tha's wearing 'em.

Keith (*shouting*) *No!*

(*Singing*)   I kept a copy of the coupon
In me other pair of trousers.
Now they've gone and disappeared
Me pitch is well and truly queered.
I'm sure I sent the soddin' coupon
But for God's sake, where's the copy?
Have a look beneath the bed
I'm going out me flippin' head.
The cowin' coupon's in a cupboard
Or it's stuck behind the sofa.
But it's gotta be somewhere
It didn't melt into thin air.
Maybe I'm mad and I imagined
That I posted it, but didn't.
Just like me to go and cock it up,
Oh look! — It's in me pocket... (*He takes out the coupon*)

Viv We were in such a state we couldn't even count. So we sent for an expert opinion.

George enters

Keith What do you reckon, George? (*He shows George the coupon*)
George Tha's seven draws all right.
Keith What did I tell you, Goldie?
Chorus Late kick-off!
George No, wait.

Chorus (*singing*) Huddersfield, one — Bristol Rovers, one!

George (*speaking*) Eight draws!
Keith Yer, what?

No. 11 Two Rooms

George (*singing*)   Eight draws!
You've got 'em all, eight draws!
Luck was a bitch, but now you're rich
She's bloody Santa Claus.

Two rooms
You'd easy fill two rooms,
If you get all that brass in cash
As you will, one presumes.

Two rooms
You'll need the extra space,
Else where on earth d'ya keep the stuff?
You'll need a bigger place.

Two yachts
Two yachts, a summer cruise!
There's one for you and me — and Viv,
And one to tow the booze.

Two wives to help spend all that dosh
Keep Viv for ev'ryday use and
The other one for posh.

If you laid ev'ry one pound note
End to end, I tell yer then
You'd reach from here right to the moon

Keith
George To the moon and back again.

Keith Two homes
We'll need to buy two homes,
A mansion and a bungalow
To house the garden gnomes.

Two fags
Give me a pair of snout
I'll start to light two fags at once
In case one should go out.

Two beds
Two beds — a "yours" and "mine"
Or one for kip and one that's just
For "How's yer father".
George Fine!
Keith To hell!
Me boss can go to hell!
I'll thumb me nose at him and hold
Two fingers up as well.

Act I, Scene 9

George busily calculates on a piece of paper

George   If you stuck this lot on yer scales,
                      Reckon it would weigh two ton
Keith   And if we blow the flippin' lot
Keith
Young Viv }   We're gonna have two tons of fun.

Young Viv   Two lavs
                      There'll be no need for queues.
                      'Cept now we're toffs we can't say, "lavs"
                      We'll have to call them, "loos".

                      Two loos,
                      Two loos, so you can choose
                      To use the one for number ones
                      And one for number twos.

                      Toulouse,
                      Toulouse-Lautrec, he's great,
                      We'll have his painting on the wall.
George   Get him to decorate.

George
Keith }   Two this
                      Two that, two ev'rything,
                      As happy as two pigs in muck
                      Just like a queen and king.

Young Viv   Two jokers
                      What a pair of fools,
                      Two hours we've sat waiting now
                      And no man from the pools.

George
Keith }   Two rooms
                      We're gonna need two rooms,
                      Two rooms to keep the money in
                      We're gonna need — two rooms.

The Lights fade on the main scene, with the spotlight remaining on Viv

   George exits

Viv   Two days
                      No visit, not a call,
                      By then we thought he'd never sent
                      The coupon after all.

The music continues

Voice (*speaking, off stage*) Is Mr Keith Nicholson here?
Young Viv Keith, it's two men. Two men from the Pools!

Scene 10

The Pools Presentation Ceremony

Bright lights come up on the Company at the presentation. Reporters, photographers and Tiller girls are among the gathering. Viv and Keith stand at the front. There is lots of champagne

No. 12 Spend Spend Spend

Viv (*singing*) All aboard the gravy train
Chorus Wave goodbye to travelling second class
All aboard the gravy train

Viv Just count the flunkies,
Queuing to kiss my arse.
Solo 1 Stick your snout into the trough,
You can jump for joy — you can blow your horn.
Solo 2 Now your rocket's taking off,
You'll have champagne over your morning cornflakes.
Viv All aboard the gravy train
Chorus Snap your fingers — someone'll bring a drink.
All aboard the gravy train.
Viv Hey, look out London,
I'm gonna paint you pink.
Solo 3 Stuff your face with caviar,
Have your fill of fur coats and feather beds.
Solo 4 All the world's your oyster bar.
And if money talks you can shout your head off.
Chorus Kicks — get your kicks.
Young Viv Bottoms up, it's all a giggle.
Chorus Kicks — get your kicks.
Keith (*ogling the Tiller girls*) Flippin' 'eck!
D'yer see that jiggle?
Chorus Kicks — get your kicks
Solo 5 Wine and dine, it's not on ration.
Chorus Kicks — get your kicks
Solo 6 Quick! It's going out of fashion.

Act I, Scene 10   33

Chorus   Now the gravy train's in the station,
                  Time to have a big celebration.
                  Time for a party,
                  Time to get your
                  Kicks — get your kicks.
                  Get your kicks.
                  Kicks — get your kicks.
                  Get your kicks.

A member of the company enters as Bruce Forsyth. He carries a giant-sized cheque

Bruce   All right, my loves?
Chorus   Kicks — get your kicks.
Bruce   I'm in charge!
Chorus   Kicks — get your kicks.
Bruce   Where are they then? Oh, is it you?
Chorus   Kicks — get your kicks
                  Get your kicks.

Bruce holds up the cheque

Bruce   Look at all this beautiful money
                  Lovely lolly — sweeter than honey.
Chorus   Pics — take your pics.
Reporters   Lift your leg up, don't be shy, love,
                  And look happy, come on, try, love.
Chorus   Pics — take your pics.
Reporters   Watch the birdie — mustn't cry, dear,
                  Make it sexy, that's the idea.
Chorus   Pics — take your pics,
                  Take your pics.
Bruce   Look at all this beautiful money,
                  Look at all this beautiful money.
Reporters   Watcha gonna do with it, love?
                  Watcha gonna do with it, love?
                  Watcha gonna do with it, love?
Young Viv   I'm gonna Spend! Spend! Spend!

                  A watch!
                  I want a watch so full of diamonds
                  You can hardly see the time.
                  I want a watch,
                  Another scotch.

A mink!
I want a mink though I'm not sure
I ever wanted mink before.
At least, I think,
I want a mink.

What does one of them cost?
I'll buy it.
What's that thingy there do?
Let's try it!

Any fad
Good or bad,
Let's go mad.

Keith A gun!
I want a gun, won't I look swish,
Now I can hunt and shoot and fish,
I want a gun,
It might be fun.

Some clubs!
I want some clubs, before I'm through
I'm gonna buy Gleneagles too.
I want some clubs
And loadsa pubs.

Is that one a cheap one?
Then scrap it
Don't look at the price tag
Just wrap it.

Keith
Young Viv Never stop
Gonna shop
Til we drop.

Keith
Young Viv
Chorus Spend spend spend!
We're gonna
Spend spend spend!
We're gonna
Spend spend spend!

Act I, Scene 10

                    We're gonna
                    Spend spend spend!
                    We're gonna
                    Spend spend spend spend
                    Spend spend spend!

Young Viv   More booze!
                    I want more booze, I want it quicker,
                    Then I'm gonna lick the liquor,
                    Offa yous
                    I want more booze.

                    The lot!
                    I want the lot with flippin' knobs on,
                    Here's two fingers to the snobs.
                    Look what I've got!
                    I've got the lot.

                    Gonna have me bath taps
                    Gold plated.
                    Gonna have me sex life
                    X-rated.

Keith   Have a ball,
Young Viv   Do it all
                    Till we fall.

Keith   Spend spend spend!
Young Viv   We're gonna,
Chorus   Spend spend spend!
                    We're gonna,
                    Spend spend spend!
                    We're gonna,
                    Spend spend spend!
                    We're gonna,
                    Spend spend spend spend spend spend!
                    Spend spend spend spend spend spend!
                    Spend spend spend spend spend spend!Spend!

Dance Break

                    Spend spend spend!
                    We're gonna

Spend spend spend!
We're gonna
Spend spend spend!
We're gonna
Spend spend spend!
We're gonna
Spend!
Spend!
Spend spend spend,
We're gonna
Spend spend spend spend!
We're gonna
Spend spend spend spend spend spend!
Spend spend spend spend spend spend!
Spend spend spend spend spend spend!
Spend spend spend spend spend spend!
Spend!
Spend spend spend spend spend spend spend spend!
Spend!

ACT II

Scene 1

The Miners' Arms

A banner above the bar reads "Welcome home Viv and Keith." There is a big sack of mail behind the bar

The Lights comes up on the Company, including George and the Pub Landlady, as Castleford residents drinking in the bar. Viv stands out of the scene as a narrator for her memories and remains on stage throughout the Act

No. 13 The Miners' Arms

Viv
Chorus (*singing*) Castleford folk,
Look after each other.
Castleford folk,
Look after their own.
Castleford folk,
Are just like a fam'ly.
You'll never have to be alone
With Castleford folk around.
Welcome back home now
Viv and Keith.
Welcome back home to
Where you belong.
Let us be just like one big happy fam'ly
The money won't have changed 'em
It won't have changed them one little bit.
They're Castleford folk like us
They're Castleford folk like — —

Young Viv and Keith enter. They are dressed in extremely flashy clothes

Woman Bloody 'ell.
Drinker (*pushing his mate*) Go on, lad.

Chorus	Give us three cheers,
	For Viv and Keith.
	Hip, hip, hooray! stay
	Where you belong.
	Couldn't have happened to a nicer couple
	We hope it makes you happy.
	We hope it makes you happy as hell
	You're Castleford folk like us
	You're Castleford folk like us.
Keith	We'll take care of thee
	We'll take care of thee.
	The drinks are on us
	We'll pick up the tab.
	We're going to get 'em in
	Drink all that you want
	Light, bitter or brown,
	Drambuie, port or gin,
	We'll take care of thee
	We'll take care of thee.

There is a mad stampede for the bar

Chorus	All aboard the gravy train,
	Fill your boots, be quick before booze runs out
	All aboard the gravy train.
Man	And mine's a brandy — —
	Why not? It's costing nowt.
Chorus	Let's get arseholed while it's there
	We all work so hard, we deserve a bash,
	They've got loads of cash to spare.
Woman	And it serves them right for both being flashy.

Solo 1 (*speaking*) Viv and Keith!
All Viv and Keith!

Viv ⎫ (*singing*) Nicholsons! The jammy bleeders
Girls ⎭ Jammy bleeders — that is all

Solo 2	Now they think they're summat special
	They'll be riding for a fall.
Chorus	They're riding for a fall.

George (*speaking*) While you were in London, you've had some post.
Viv A sackful of beggin' letters.

Act II, Scene 1

George dumps the big sack of mail at Keith's and Viv's feet

The Lights close in around Keith, Young Viv and George. Young Viv and Keith begin to open some of the letters

   On another part of the stage, a man dressed as a sweet, little, old granny enters into a tight spotlight

Granny (*singing*)Yesterday my wee cat, my little kitty died
          Run down and killed,
          And, dearie, how I cried.
          Had her seventeen years
          I'm eighty-two today.
          But what will I do now pussy's gone away?
          I've no-one to talk to without him around.
          I'd buy another cat but I need eighty pound.
          Oh, kitty,
          Poor, kitty,
          Who'll take care of me?
          Who'll take care of me now you've gone?

Young Viv (*speaking*; *moved*) We'll have to send her the money.
Viv But the man from the Pools put us right.

   A man from the Pools enters and snatches the letter out of Young Viv's hand

Pools Man (*singing*)   They're written by pros,
          They're all on the scrounge
          They're conning you if they can
          That little old dear's
          A dangerous crook
          And what's more she's a man!

In the spotlight, the granny takes of her disguise and looks like a menacing fraudster

Fraudster (*speaking; to the Pools man*) Keep out of it, you!

   The Fraudster exits

The spotlight fades and the main lighting is restored

Pools Man (*singing*) I'll take care of these.
George Daughter, oh, daughter
Don't she take after me?
Please put an end to my frettin'
All I am askin's
Has tha' made up tha mind,
How much thy dad'll be gettin'?

Young Viv (*speaking*) You're not gettin' a penny.
George Remember how I brought you up from a little bairn!
Young Viv I do. That's why you're not gettin' a penny.
George Thanks for your honesty, love. (*Aside, to a friend*) She'll come round.

Chorus (*singing*) Booze! Down the booze!
George Seeing stars?
I'm seeing comets!
Chorus Booze!
Down the booze!
Girl Won't be long before he vomits.
George 'Eck! The wife is feeling frisky.
Chorus Booze!
Down the booze!
George Mary, quick!
Gonna need
Another whisky.

Landlady (*speaking*) Here's your bill, love. (*Passing Keith the bar bill*) It's gonna cost you a quid or two.
Keith Bloody 'ell! It's six months' wages. Lucky I'm not earning them anymore!

(*Singing*) Behold! My brand new cheque book
Behold! My gold-nibbed Parker fountain pen
As used by gentlemen.

Behold! I'm like an artist
Behold! I sign my name like Mozart did
Behold! Two hundred quid!

Everyone cheers

Man Nicholsons! The jammy bleeders,
Woman Jumped up bigheads — that is clear.

Act II, Scene 1   41

Man   Truth to tell, I never liked 'em,
Woman   Even so, we'll drink their beer.
Man   Yes, we will drink their beer.
Chorus   Booze! Down the booze!
Man (*speaking*) Cheers, Keith!
Chorus (*singing*) Booze! Down the booze!
Young Viv (*speaking*) Who's that?
Chorus (*singing*) Booze! Down the booze
Keith (*speaking*) Never seen him before in me life.
Chorus (*singing*) Booze! Down the booze!
Young Viv (*speaking*) I've not seen half of these before.
Keith (*singing*) Just look at 'em, will yer!
                     Get drunker and sillier,
                     And as I look round here,
                     There's hardly a face that's remotely familiar.

                     Pushing, shoving, shouting in the streets
                     Dust-ups, bust-ups, all a bit too much.
                     People think you'll be an easy touch.
                     You meet old friends,
                     They make no sound.
                     There's nowt to say,
                     There's no common ground.
                     The world has changed,
                     For you and me,
                     And nothing in it ever can be the same.

Jealous Woman (*speaking*) Jammy pig!

Chorus   Get a new home now,
                     Viv and Keith.
                     Get a new home,
                     Somewhere you belong.
Stranger   How does it feel, like — winning all that money?
Keith   Like being in a freak show,
                     And starring me, the king of the freaks,
                     We're Castleford folk no more.
Chorus   You're Castleford folk no more.

A furious brawl breaks out among the freeloaders

Viv   Laughing, talking, dancing in the streets,
                     Sing songs, ding dongs, dominoes and darts.
                     Front doors open wide, like people's hearts,

                A better time
                Went by so quick
                Or is the mem'ry,
                Playing a trick?

During the following, the Lights close in around Young Viv and Keith

  In darkness, the Company exits

Young Viv }   The world has changed
Keith   }   For you and me,
                And nothing in it ever can be the same.

Young Viv (*speaking*) Keith?
Keith Yes, love?

No.13a Take Me Away

Young Viv (*singing*)   Let's get a car.
Keith (*speaking*) Yer what?
Young Viv (*singing*) Buy me a car.
Keith (*speaking*) A car!
Young Viv (*singing*) Summat that's big and noisy and flash, just like what we are.
                Pink Chevrolet.
Keith (*speaking*) Pink Viv!!
Viv (*singing*)   Pink Chevrolet!
                That's what I want.
                A bloody great pink American car.

  A "Chevrolet Impala" car with a bikini-clad model on the bonnet comes in

Young Viv sings on an "ah"

Keith (*speaking*) Is it to your liking, Goldie?
Young Viv   I think it is.

  (*Singing*)   Take me away.
Viv   Take me away.
Young Viv   Off to the place,
                That I wanna go ter
Viv   Far, far away,
Young Viv   Hide me away,
Viv   Hide me away.
Young Viv   Let's go to Garforth
                There we will be OK.

Act II, Scene 2

An Estate Agent enters

Keith
Viv
Young Viv   (*speaking*) Garforth!
Estate Agent

SCENE 2

Immediately following

During the following, in the darkness the Company enter as the people of Garforth

No.14 Garforth

Estate Agent (*singing*) Garforth!
                    Is only ten miles away.
                    But across the social divide
                    A gulf a thousand miles wide.
Young Viv   Garforth!
                    If it's as good as they say,
                    Then to Garforth we will go forth.
Estate Agent   The Shangri-la of the North.
Young Viv   Garforth!
                    We're going way upper-class,
                    And if anyone doubts us
                    We'll show them our brass.
Estate Agent   There's the new estate …
Young Viv   We can hardly wait.

Full lighting comes up on the interior of a new home in Garforth. Surrounding the interior, there is a strip of lawn. The people of Garforth mow the lawn in neat straight lines

All   We/You will be happy, in Garforth,
Young Viv   Where our money won't cause a buzz.
All   We/You will be happy in Garforth,
Young Viv   They've all got a woman who does,
                    'Cos it's considered demeaning,
                    To do your own cleaning,
                    In Garforth.

Keith   Garforth!
I can't believe this is real,
Ev'ryone's so terribly nice,
Their kids would never get lice.

Garforth!
Is what is known as genteel.
They're dead bleedin' posh when they talk,
They eat their cake with a fork.
Garforth!
Nobody works down the mine.
They're too busy all
Knocking back fancy French wine,
Eating, if you please
Pineapple with cheese.
Young Viv (*speaking*) Vol-au-vents!

Estate Agent   You will be happy in Garforth
Where a life can never be hard.
You will be happy in Garforth
Keith   The bog isn't in the backyard
Estate Agent   I should think not!
Instead the grass is a-growing
They never stop mowing,
In Garforth.

The Estate Agent starts to show Young Viv and Keith round the interior of the home

Estate Agent (*speaking*) Mr Nicholson, Mrs Nicholson.
   (*Singing*)   Have a look at our show house,
Detached and enormous.
Through here, and now maybe you'd like a,
Peek at the kitchen;
The builders inform us
It's genuine, solid Formica.

(*Speaking*) Is it to your liking, madam, sir?
Young Viv We'll take it! All the furniture and the bits and pieces, the lot. (*To Keith*) It's huge.
Keith Viv! Look at size of that garden! You could fit a hundred head of cattle in it.
Young Viv And I know what to call it.

Act II, Scene 2   45

Young Viv ⎫
Keith   ⎬ (*together*) *Ponderosa!*
Viv   ⎭

The middle-class neighbours react to one another, then continue to mow their lawns

Neighbours   Garforth!
                 Is like its own little niche,
                 I'm afraid their faces don't fit.
                 They're both as vulgar as shit.
                 Upstarts!
                 The pair are so *nouveau riche*;
                 Flashy, trashy, brash as they come,
                 They stick out like a sore thumb.
                 Standards
                 Are what we try to maintain.
                 If you let standards drop values go down the drain.
                 See the neighbourhood,
                 Buggered up for good.

Young Viv   I've got a house that is bigger than yours,
                 Buy all me gear at the fanciest stores;
                 That is the thing really sticks in your craws.
                 Well, if you don't like it — then lump it.
                 I've got an au pair, a nanny, a maid.
                 Look at me sofa, Italian suede
                 I drive a Chevrolet, I made the grade,
                 So don't show your face or — I'll thump it.
Neighbours   Strumpet!

Viv   We'll be unhappy in Garforth,
                 Where they're always cleaning their cars.
                 We'll be unhappy in Garforth,
                 You'd think we just landed from Mars.
                 When people turn up their noses,
                 It's no bed of roses
                 If they keep on making a fuss,
                 We'll be unhappy in Garforth.

Viv   ⎫
Keith   ⎬ And we will make damn sure that
Young Viv ⎭

                    Garforth
                    For certain
                    Behind its net curtain
                    Is bloody unhappy with us!

The Lights close in around Keith and Young Viv

   The Estate Agent exits

In the darkness, the Company regroup as guests at a party

Viv But we did make some new friends — like the Bank Manager.

The Bank Manager, suited, sidles up to Keith and takes him aside. The Bank Manger has documents

No. 14a Garforth Coda

Keith (*Speaking*) Bloody 'ell.
Bank Manager (*singing*) The bank is worried, Mr Nicholson
                    The level of your spending is the
                    Cause for some concern, you seem to
                    Think you've cash to burn and while your
                    Win was rather handsome,
                    You've been paying a king's ransom,
                    At a level not agreed
                    On things that you don't even need.
Keith   So what? So what? I'm very rich.
Bank Manager But not in credit, as my
                    Letter did spell out to you.
Keith   Yeah, well, I never read it.
Bank Manager And a will, dear Mr Nicholson
                    A will to keep things tidy.
                    Sign along the dotted line, it needs a
                    Signature — please, sign it!

Keith signs

   The Bank Manager exits

Full lighting comes up on a wild and sleazy party at Viv's and Keith's house

Young Viv (*speaking*) Party time!

Act II, Scene 2   47

Viv   Garforth,
                   We put the place on the map,
                   Went berserk and drank ourselves daft.
                   Oh, how we laughed and we laughed.
                   Rave ups!
                   The booze were always on tap,
                   Ev'ery night from dusk until dawn,
                   And they're still mowing the lawn!
Chorus   You will be happy in Garforth.

There is a ring at the doorbell and Viv opens the door

   A Policeman enters

The music continues to underscore

Policeman Sorry Viv, we've had some complaints again, about the noise.
Young Viv I'm very sorry officer but it's a very special occasion.
Policeman It was your anniversary last time.
Young Viv Well this time — it's our Sammy's birthday.
Policeman Who's Sammy?
Young Viv Our cocker spaniel. (*She hands the policeman a drink*)
Policeman Well, let's just try and keep it down a bit.

The Policeman joins the party

Young Viv Pulled a copper!

Viv (*singing*)   Parties,
                       That never came to an end.
                       We got swept along on the tide,
                       And taking us for a ride.
                       Cronies!
                       But not one genuine friend,
                       Only toffs and upper-class tarts,
                       Sex-mad and all pissed as farts.
Chorus   You will be happy in Garforth

Keith begins dancing with a woman

The music continues to underscore

Young Viv What's going on 'ere then?

Keith This is Mrs Thompson, luv. She lives at number twenty-four.
Woman Please call me Belinda.
Young Viv I know what to call you. Come here, you scrubber!

Young Viv springs at the woman. Keith pulls her away

Keith She weren't doin' nowt, love!
Young Viv Get out me house. The lot of you. Piss off!
Keith It's a party, love!
Young Viv I saw you!
Keith It's a bloody party!

Young Viv moves towards the exit

Where you going now?
Young Viv I bloody hate it here.
Keith Bloody 'ell fire!

Keith follows Young Viv

The Guests exit

The Lights close in around Keith and Young Viv

We weren't really doing anything, love.

No. 14b Take Me Away

Young Viv You're sleeping on your own tonight!
Keith Come on, love.

Viv (*singing*) Take me away,
Take me away.
Let's plan a big
American trip.
Let's fly there today.

A stewardess enters, wheeling a drinks trolley

Stewardess US of A
US of A
Young Viv Off to the States
To live it up.

Act II, Scene 2   49

Keith   Is it far?
Young Viv   Dunno.
Stewardess   Land of the free,
                   So much to see,
                   Broadway and baseball, Beverly Hills,
                   Elvis, the White House, so many thrills,
                   Golden Gate Bridge, the Statue of Liberty.

A doorman enters, carrying Young Viv's and Keith's bags

Full lighting comes up on a hotel room in New York

  The stewardess exits

Doorman   This is New York,
                   Mind where you walk.
                   Don't go to Harlem
                   Or Central Park.
                   Don't go no damn place,
                   After it's dark.
                   I guess you come from Scotland
                   The way you talk.

The doorman carries the bags into the hotel room

The music continues to underscore

Keith No, we're from England, Garforth near Leeds
Doorman Leeds, huh? So, you know the Beatles?
Keith Us and the Beatles? We're like that!
Doorman Yeh? My kid sister nearly killed herself over them. I'd like to murder those long-haired bastards.
Keith Well, you know, we're not *that* close.

Young Viv and Keith now admire their hotel room

Young Viv Look at all them lights! I think this is what they call King-size. Like someone else I know. (*She lies on the bed provocatively*) Make me sing *The Star-Spangled Banner*.

Keith spots the television and turns it on

Keith Bloody 'ell! It's in colour!

Keith gets a drink and settles down to watch. He continues to drink heavily

Scene 3

The same, immediately following

No. 15 Drinking in America

Young Viv (*singing*) Dear all, we've had a smashing time
Or "smashed time" — if you get me drift.
The other day we goes to climb
The Empire State — can't find a lift.
A great hotel room in New York,
A mini-bar beside the bed.
We got so tight we couldn't walk,
Stayed in and watched TV instead.

The hotel staff all smile at you,
So friendly, God, it makes yer sick.
They bring your food and drink up to
Your room — it's like a five-star nick.
We did get homesick one night so,
We found a phoney English bar.
All full of Scots and Irish though,
All pissed, who do they think they are?

We've been drinking in America,
Drinking in America.

We're in this bar — both drunk as 'ell,
Some woman sits starin' at Keith.
I think she fancies him, get jealous,
So I smack her in the teeth.
I get a shock — her head's like wood.
The barman sits her there for fun,
She's just a dummy, in't it good?
And now she's not the only one.

There's such amazing sights we've seen,
There's always something on the box.
You're cared for well — each drink has been
Served like our marriage — "On the rocks".
I miss the way life used to be,
Done nowt but drink since we've been here
I'd love a decent cuppa tea,
Keith says he misses proper beer.

Act II, Scene 4   51

>   We've been drinking in America,
>   Drinking in America
>   Drinking in America
>   Drinking in America.

The Lights go down on the main scene and focus on Viv. The music continues

Keith exits

SCENE 4

Viv (*singing*)   Back to an empty house, just us
                         The kids are all away at school.
                         Nowt's changed as far as I can see,
                         Oh, Viv, you've been a bloody fool.
                         This travel game — it's not our game
                         A total waste of time and brass,
                         'Cos ev'rywhere looks much the same
                         Seen through the bottom of a glass.

The Lights come up on Young Viv in her bedroom

Florrie, a housekeeper, enters and brings Young Viv a cup of tea and a whisky

Florrie Hallo, love. Here's your tea, Viv.
Viv Me housekeeper, Florrie.
Young Viv Ta, Florrie.
Viv So life carried on like that. Boozin', rowin' spendin', doin' nowt. Drifting further and further apart. Until one day ...

Keith enters holding a canary in a cage

Florrie He's home early.

Florrie exits

Young Viv Yeah. Pub catch fire?
Keith No — I picked up a bird.
Young Viv So, what else is new?
Keith No, no. Come and have a look.

No. 16 Canary in a Cage

(*Singing*) It happened once upon a time,
The story of a small canary.
A Yorkshire fancy all alone in a shop
Who never thought that he were owt but ordinary.

One day a miner comes and says,
Hey little bird, I'll be your master.
I'm gonna take yer down below where it's dark,
And you will sing there as a warning of disaster.

Hear the canary sing his song,
And hear the happy news he's giving.
For while he sings, there's nothing wrong,
And you and I can go on living.

For many years he carried on,
For many long years like a miner.
And everybody down the pit, they would see him,
And agree that there were no canary finer.

The music continues to underscore

Viv Truth to tell, it looked like it were about to snuff it. But he tended it with so much love. Hardly had the time to booze.

No. 17 Canary (part 2)

Keith (*singing*) You gotta feed 'em on green food
And seed mix,
Or soft food,
When they're still chicks.

I'm gonna buy him a tall cage,
'Cos he might
Need wing-room to
Stand upright.

But, singing alone,
Ain't much of a fate.
And me, I'm like him.
I want my mate.

Act I, Scene 4   53

    (*Speaking*) I do love you, Viv. You know I'd never do anything to hurt you.
Young Viv You haven't touched me in months.

Tentatively Keith and Young Viv touch and than finally embrace

Viv (*singing*)   But though the scars of love
                     Always remain.
                     They're worth the pain of it.
                     Love that tears the soul,
                     And breaks the heart
                     Is all a part of it.

                     You wipe away your tears,
                     But one thing never disappears
                     The wound that time won't heal
                     That no one sees, but you
                     Will always feel.
                     And so it hurts, but all is fair,
                     We all must bear
                     The scars of love.

The music continues to underscore

Viv After that I were mad keen on animals. Pets, couldn't have enough of them. Keith really loved horses. Well backin' 'em. One day he drove to Wetherby for the races.
Keith See you later, love, I'm gonna be late. (*etc.*)
Young Viv See you later …

    Keith exits

The Lights close in on Viv

Viv And I had a lie-in. We had been up all night. And so when there was a knock at the door, I thought it was Keith back. But it wasn't, it was a policeman.

    A Policeman enters

The Lights come up on Young Viv and a Policeman

Young Viv What's up this time?
Policeman Viv. Mrs Nicholson, there's been a car accident. (*He bursts into tears*)

Viv (*singing*)	I remember the way they told me he had died.
	Knew it were bad,
	That copper bloody cried.
	Pussyfooted around,
	Then blurted out …
Policeman	Keith's dead.
Viv	They pumped me with drugs,
	And put me straight to bed.
	Collected his wallet and his keys and comb.
	Identified his body,
	Cried and then went home.
	Oh, darling.
	Poor darling.
	Who'll take care of me.
	Who'll take care of me now tha's gone?

The Policeman exits

Full lighting comes up

The Company enters, including George and Viv's mother, as mourners at Keith's funeral

Young Viv moves DS

Scene 5

Immediately following

No. 18 Who's Gonna Love Me

Young Viv (*singing*)	I search for traces of you on the pillow,
	The smell of you, an eyelash or a hair.
	I do believe at least you really loved me,
	I trusted you to stay,
	Now you're not there.
	And I wonder, who's gonna love me?
	Who's gonna love me?
	Who's gonna love me now you're gone?
Viv	And I wonder, who's gonna love me?
	Who's gonna love me?
	Who's gonna love me now?

Act II, Scene 5   55

Viv   ⎫ I howl, I cry, I know I won't recover,
Young Viv   ⎬ You're gone and part of me has gone with you.
                    There's people here — and yet the house is empty
                    And you must know it's true,
                    I'm empty too.

Viv   And I wonder, who's gonna love me?
                    Who's gonna love me?
                    Who's gonna love me now you're gone?
Young Viv   And I wonder, who's gonna love me?
                    Who's gonna love me?
                    Who's gonna love me now?

                    No-one to lie beside.
Viv   No-one to help me hide.
Young Viv   No-one to know me well.
Viv   No-one to give me hell.
Young Viv   No-one to dress up for.
Viv   No-one to kiss no more.
Young Viv   No-one to share the fun.
Viv
Young Viv   You were my special one

                    And I wonder, who's gonna love me?
                    Who's gonna love me?
                    Who's gonna love me now you're gone?
                    And I wonder, who's gonna love me?
                    Who's gonna love me?
                    Who's gonna love me now you're gone?

Viv's mother and Viv's dad, George, approach Young Viv at the "grave-side"

Mother Oh, luv.
George No good grieving, lass. It happens to us all sometime.
Mother Tha' callous bugger! It's her husband!
George Well, I'll have to go sometime.
Mother I wish they'd bleedin' hurry up and take thee.
Viv Then the men in suits came to give their condolences.

Viv's mother and George move away to join the other mourners

  A Bank Manager and Tax Man enter

No.19 Dance of the Suits

Bank Manger The bank is sorry, Mrs Nicholson,
We'd like to pay our most sincere
Respects to you today.
But now it's time for you to pay,
You see, the Nicholson estate is in a —
Well, it's in a state.
Therefore the books are balanced thus,
All that was yours belongs to us.

Tax Man Will you accept heart-felt condolences
From all at Inland Revenue?
We're working for Her Majesty,
We've come here on the cadge.
You see, the Queen must get her due,
And it's my duty to collect it,
Re: the records we have showing us,
The duty that you're owing.

Bank Manager⎫ Commence by confiscating
Tax Man   ⎭ Ev'ry piece of correspondence.
Showing places dates and names
That might substantiate our claims.
Take possession of the documents
The passports and the papers.
Now it's clearly time to compensate
The Nicholson Estate.

We are experts in the field
Of small print — big words.
They're the weapons that we wield
The small print — big words.

Or should we say
Voluminous verbosity
And microscopic typographical.
Communication that'll
Keep you in your station.
We can see this situation
Is confounding and confusing.
Does this explanation clear it up?

Act II, Scene 5   57

Young Viv ⎫ Well, no …
Bank Manager ⎭
Tax Man   We're glad to hear it!
Mourners   They are experts in the field
                    Of small print — big words.
                    They will keep the facts concealed
                    With small print — big words.

The Tax Man and the Bank Manger join the other mourners

Young Viv Keith, what have you done?
Viv He'd signed a will. A stupid will. The bank controlled all the money. I had to take 'em to court. Meanwhile — the vultures gathered.

No. 19a Pieces of Me

(*Singing*)   Look at me now
                    I'm broken in two
                    Shattered and battered,
                    Bitter and blue.
                    Here come the vultures
                    They wanna dine,
                    All stood in line for
                    Pieces of me.

                    Now there are guys
                    Dressed up in their suits.
                    Spelling out trouble
                    Legal disputes,
                    Look at 'em gather
                    They're all the same
                    All got a claim on
                    Pieces of me ...

Chorus   Ev'rybody wants a piece of the action,
                    Ev'rybody wants a slice of the cake.
                    Ev'rybody will demand satisfaction,
                    Ev'rybody's on the make.

                    Ev'rybody wants a lend of a shilling,
                    Ev'rybody wants a shake of the stick.
                    Ev'rybody will be making a killing,
                    Everybody's on the nick.

Viv (*speaking*) Some lying tart from way back said Keith owed her child maintenance.

A Tart enters

Tart (*singing*) Keith took advantage of me,
  Put me in the fam'ly way.
  Left me to rear his baby,
  Now you're gonna bleeding pay!
Young Viv (*speaking*) Tha' lying cow! Tha's had more pricks than a pin cushion!
Tart Now you're gonna bleeding pay!
Young Viv Come here!
Viv And his family took a private action against me 'cos his uncle Frank died in crash an' all.

Keith's mum and dad enter

Mum ⎫ Uncle's dead
Dad ⎭ We're grieving too.
  But compensate us,
  We'll pull through.
Young Viv (*speaking*) Liars!

Viv (*singing*) Distant relations
  Look at 'em come.
  Sniffin' around for
  One little crumb.

Grandad enters

Young Viv (*speaking*) Who are you?!

Grandad (*singing*) I raised Keith
  Just like a son.
  Now he's gone
  And I've got none.
George ⎫ Two rooms
Mother ⎭ They've emptied out two rooms

Viv (*speaking*) Even local council were on the scrounge.

A Council Man enters

Act II, Scene 5   59

Council Man   The council wants
                  Some recompense.
                  His car destroyed
                  Municipal fencing.
          Municipal fencing.

Young Viv exits

Viv   A little bit here
                  A little bit there.
                  That's how they tear off
                  Pieces of me.
                  Yes and so it hurts
                  Now I'm alone
                  Picked to the bone.
                  Nowt left to show,
                  I watch them go.
                  Pieces of me.

Tart   Keith took advantage of me
                  Put me in the fam'ly way.
                  Left me to rear his baby.
                  Now you're gonna bleedin' pay!
Mum ⎫   Uncle's dead
Dad ⎭   We're grieving too.
                  But compensate us
                  We'll pull through.
Grandad   I raised Keith
                  Just like a son,
                  Now he's gone
                  And I've got none.
Council Man   The council wants
                  Some recompense.
                  His car destroyed
                  Municipal fencing.
                  Ev'rybody wants a piece of the action,
Viv   ⎫   Ev'rybody wants a slice of the cake.
Chorus ⎭   Ev'rybody will demand satisfaction,
                  Ev'rybody's on the make.
Viv   Here for the will,
                  The world and his wife.

People I've hardly,
Seen in me life.
Out of the woodwork
Look at 'em crawl
Grabbing at all the
Piece of me
Pieces of me.

The Lights go down on the Company

A spotlight comes up on a Judge

Judge I award the plaintiff the sum of thirty-four thousand pounds.
Viv Six bleedin' years deciding that! Thirty-four grand! Still, not bad. Now, what could I buy with that? I know!

There is a lighting change

The spotlight goes out on the Judge and he exits

Scene 6

No.20 A Brand New Husband

The Lights come up on Young Viv and New Husband 3

Husband 3 beats Viv

Young Viv   A brand new husband,
Though I'm no beginner.
A brand new husband,
I can sure pick a winner.
First date, all charm — you can't ask for more,
Next time, it's kapow! And you're on the floor.
Split lip, black eye and a broken jaw,
From your brand new husband.

Husband 3 (*speaking*) Oh. I'm so sorry, forgive me, love!
Viv Apparently, it were all a mistake.
Husband 3 Let's get you to hospital.
Viv He proposed to me in Casualty. Well I told him —
Young Viv Yes.
Viv Yeah! I could smack her one meself! A week after the wedding, I took out a separation order …

Act II, Scene 6   61

Husband 3 Viv!
Viv A month later …
Husband 3 Viv! I only do it 'cos I love you! …

Young Viv (*singing*) It's no wonder I went,
                         Nearly out my head.
                         We all dream Mr Right
                         Is the man we'll wed.
                         But we wake up beside
                         Mr Shite instead.
                         He's your brand new husband.

Husband 3 exits and Husband 4 enters

                         A brand new husband
                         We all need adoring,
                         A brand new husband
                         What a pity he's boring.
                         When we're in bed me head starts to ache
                         'Cos love's just a mess, you don't want to make.
                         But given time you learn how to fake (*She fakes an orgasm*)
                         For your brand new husband.
                         But it won't be too long
                         Till you've had a think.
Young Viv ⎫   There is little love lost
Husband 4 ⎬   We are on the blink.
Young Viv ⎭   It's another divorce
                         Never lost a wink
                         Lost another husband.

Husband 4 exits and Husband 5 enters

                         A brand new husband
                         Am I sounding bitter?
                         A brand new husband
                         You can't call me a quitter.
                         Forget him shooting up in the loo.
                         Forgive him his beating you black and blue,
                         As long as he tells you.

Husband 5   I love you,
              I do, I really and truly do. (*He beats Young Viv*)

George enters. He looks as he did when Viv was fifteen

George   He touched your thingies?
Tha's a bag and a whore,
Filth muck and rubbish!
You won't see him no more.

How could you shame me?
I'll take care of thee!
Now you're gettin' what for,
Thou art no daughter of mine!

Young Viv breathes painfully and noisily

Husband 5 (*speaking*) Why are you making that noise?
Young Viv You cracked my ribs with that kung fu kick.
Viv He were a big fan of Bruce Lee.
Husband 5 You make me feel a right low bastard. (*Brightly*) Well, you won't have to put up with it any more. I've just taken my tablets, the whole bottle ...

Husband 5 exits

Young Viv (*singing*) So it's overdose time
I've no luck with men.
Soon the ambulance comes
You're in trouble then.
And they say he'll be fine
But you mourn again.
Young Viv
Viv } And you mourn again ...
Young Viv And you mourn again ...
Mourn for a brand new husband.

Viv (*speaking*) Down to me last ten grand. 'Ey! But that were still enough to see me through happily to the end of my days. — Was it 'eck!

There is a lighting change

No. 21 Spent

A glitzy chorus, with show girls etc., enter

Chorus (*singing*) All aboard the gravy train
Wave goodbye to travelling second class.
All aboard the gravy train
Just ...

Act II, Scene 6

Viv (*speaking*) No! Bugger off! Bugger off! You too! Get out of it! No, it weren't like that at all! I was determined this time things were going to be different.

The Chorus exit

Viv
Young Viv } Invest!
Young Viv   Invest the money, make a mint.
             Never again will I be skint,
             If I invest.
Viv   Are you impressed?
Young Viv A shop!

Viv (*speaking*) So I bought a shop.

Rails of dresses are wheeled on and other clothes shop objects are brought on

(*Singing*)   I'll buy a shop — I like boutiques.
             It's full of mice — a roof that leaks,
             My little shop.
Viv   It starts to flop
Young Viv I can wear the clothes so,
             Let's stock up,
             Ev'rything in size ten.
Viv   A cock-up!
             Half the dough,
             Watch it go,
             Cheerio!

Bailiffs enter

Bailiffs (*speaking*) Mrs Nicholson!

Young Viv
Viv   } (*singing*) In debt!
Bailiffs

Bailiffs Now, I'm in debt and I'm in deep,
             When you let friends have stuff so cheap.
             What do you get?
             You get in debt.
             Go broke.

Young Viv	I'm going broke and half insane,
	I've seen me dream go down the drain,
	Or up in smoke.
Viv	A flippin' joke,
	Never understood for
	One second,
	Why it didn't work how
	I reckoned ...
	Made a hash
	Of the cash
	In a flash.

The Bailiffs cross the stage carrying away various objects. When all has been cleared they exit

Young Viv }	Spent, spent, spent!
Viv	All of it
	Spent, spent, spent!
	All of it
	Spent, spent, spent!
	All of it
	Spent, spent, spent!
	All of it.
Young Viv	Spent, spent, spent!
	Spent, spent, spent!
Viv	Spent, spent, spent, spent!
	Spent, Spent — —
Young Viv }	
Viv	Spent.

Viv's son and daughter enter. They carry on the caged canary

Daughter } (*speaking*) Mam, mam, they've taken all our toys!
Son
Young Viv And mine, luv. And mine! Look, what they've left us. This were your dad's.

Act II, Scene 7   65

                No. 22 Canary in a Cage (Reprise)

Young Viv   It happened once upon a time,
                This story of a small canary,
                A little Goldie and she lived in a cage,
                And never thought that she were owt but ordinary.

                Until the time she found her mate,
                A Yorkshire of the finest feather.
                And she and he broke free and flew from the cage,
                And what a time they had both flying high together.

                You gotta feed 'em on green food
                And seed mix,
                And soft food when
                They're still chicks.
                It's time for me to go back to
                Me old cage,
                And start over
                At my age.

Young Viv (*speaking*) Come on you two. Off to bed.

Young Viv and the children exit, with the caged bird

Viv (*singing*)   'Cos singing alone
                Ain't much of a fate,
                And me I'm like him
                I want my mate.

The Lights dim and close in around Viv

                        Scene 7

Immediately following

                No. 23 Mother, Oh, Mother

Viv So, I'd lost everything. Me money, me youth, me men. Years went by and I learned to do without fellers, because, well, sex is like dusting, i'nt it? — if you don't do if for years you don't notice the difference. Till this one feller came among.

    A Stranger enters and is caught in Viv's light

Stranger Hey, Goldie, where are you?
Viv I'd seen him a couple of times. Call me an optimist or what, but I did think to meself — could he be husband number six?
Stranger I can't see a blindin' thing!

Viv (*singing*)   The moment I saw him,
                     I wondered — what if?

Young Viv enters into the darkness

Young Viv (*speaking*) Keep lookin' you're gettin' warmer!

Viv (*singing*)   Perhaps he'll be special,
                     Perhaps he'll be diff'rent.

Stranger (*speaking*) Where's the soddin' lights?
Young Viv Warmer still …

Viv (*singing*)   When I feel desire
                     By 'eck I'm a trier,
                     So is it real love, I see loomin'.

The Lights come up on Young Viv's home, as if Young Viv has switched them on

Young Viv (*speaking*) Red hot.

Viv (*singing*)   There's one way to find out
                     Upstairs in me room

Viv's daughter enters

Daughter	Mother, oh, Mother
	Who you hiding in here?
	P'raps you should get out more often.
Stranger	"Mother" she called you
	Is this some kind of joke?
Young Viv	I were a child bride you soft 'un
Stranger	Goldie, now honestly, love
	How old are thee?
Young Viv	I'm not ashamed to say,
	That I'm thirty-three.

Act II, Scene 7

Young Viv turns threateningly to her daughter

> Don't tha' say nowt, lass
> Or else tha'll get clog pie.
> Bugger off, daughter of mine.

Viv's daughter exits

> Where were we …

Viv Wherever you wander,
Wherever you roam.
Stranger I'm crazy about you!
Viv You never stop dreaming of love for a moment.

Young Viv (*speaking*) So, you don't mind older women then?

Viv (*singing*) And never stop missing,
The touching and kissing
'Cos after all we're only human.

Young Viv kneels and begins to unzip his trousers

Stranger (*speaking*) Oh, Goldie!

Viv (*singing*) We might see some action
Upstairs in me — —

Viv's son enters

Son Mother, oh, Mother
What you doing down there?
Never mind, long as you're happy.

He exits

Stranger Mother? His mother?
That great hulkin' big lad?
You said he still wore a nappy

> If you're his mother, Sue,
> You cannot fool me.
> Either he's seven
> Or you're not thirty-three!

Viv Well, there comes a time when you've got to come clean, be who and what you are. Truth be told I was forty-one by then.

Young Viv exits

Viv replaces Young Viv

I'm thirty-nine. (*To the audience*) Tell the truth, yes, but there's no need to get fanatical! (*To the Stranger*) And another thing. Me real name's Viv.

Stranger Viv? Viv Nicholson …? You're her!
  (*Singing*)   You're her! Of all the fools!
              The one who had the Pools win.
Viv (*speaking*) Are you scared of me?
Stranger (*singing*) What's worse,
              They say that you're a curse,
              Your men all wind up in a hearse.

Viv They used to call me lucky.
Stranger They call you murderess now.
Viv Is that what you think?
Stranger I don't think you killed anybody.
Viv Come here, then.
Stranger No, I'll have to be going. On early shift.

The Stranger exits

The Lights close in on Viv

Viv (*singing*)   Sod you!
              Wait till twelve o'clock, me fangs come out at night
              Sod you!
              Kiss the vampire, she's just dying for a bite!

              I do,
              Undertake to search for happiness one day.
              I do,
              Still believe that better times aren't far away.
              I do,
              Have a decent life no bastard can condemn.
              I do,
              Have me children now and I'll take care of them.
              And they'll take care of me,
              They'll take care of me.

(*Speaking*) So, that's the end of me story. And now, I'm just like everybody else. I have to work for me living.

Act II, Scene 7   69

During the song, the Company enters as the beauty salon "Salon Mystique" from the start of the musical. They are all now wearing beauty masks

No. 24 Roll Back the Years (reprise)

Viv At Salon Mystique
To tell you the truth,
We haven't the secret of eternal youth.
It's pretty good work
It's pretty good pay.
I'm older and wiser,
All right then, I'm older anyway.
Me kids are all grown
Work hard as they can.
With kids of their own
So now, I am a gran.
I've weathered the storm
The sneers and the jeers.
Now I've no desire,
To roll back the years.

(*Speaking*) Let's see how she looks now me little story's ended.

The Lights come up

Viv peels off what she and the audience believe to be Mrs Waterman's mask to reveal a beautiful young woman

Viv Bloody 'ell, Mrs Waterman? Mrs Waterman?!
Mrs Waterman (*from underneath her mask*) Over here, love! Over here!

(*Singing*)　　　Quick! Where's the mirror?
Viv　　　　　　Eh! It's Michelle bloody Pfeiffer.
Mrs Waterman　You! Bring me nearer.
Viv　　　　　　If she keeps on I will knife her!
　　　　　　　　A little beauty cream goes very far.
　　　　　　　　On second thoughts you better keep the jar
　　　　　　　　Have a nice do. I hope it piggin' rains.
　　　　　　　　Wear something blue — to go with all them veins.

Mrs Waterman (*speaking*) Here's a little something for you, luv! Bet you wish you still had all that money!
Viv I wish, I wish!

The Lights go down on Salon Mystique

The Music continues to underscore (**No. 25**)

Viv moves out of the scene into the light at the front of the stage

Viv I went back, a while ago, to our old house, where we had the win. "Excuse me, I used to live here. Do you mind if I have a look around? Thanks, love." It all came back. I thought, if we hadn't won the Pools we'd be in here now.

Young Viv and Keith enter

I was surprised how it affected me.

Viv dances with Keith, then passes him to Young Viv. They dance

Young Viv and Keith exit

That's when I had everything ...

Black-out

No. 26 Bows

The Lights come up for the Company to take their bows

No. 27 Spend Spend Spend (Reprise)

Company Spend spend spend!
We're gonna,
Spend spend spend!
We're gonna,
Spend spend spend!
We're gonna,
Spend spend spend!
We're gonna,
Spend spend spend spend spend spend!
Spend! Spend! Spend!

No. 28 Spend Spend Spend (Playout)

FURNITURE AND PROPERTY LIST

Further dressing may be added at the director's discretion.

ACT I

SCENE 1

On stage: Glossy magazine with photograph of Michelle Pfeiffer

SCENE 2

On stage: No props required

SCENE 3

On stage: Neon sign
Pictures of fifties film stars

Off stage: Ice-cream tray (**Manager**)

Personal: **Lads**: cinema tickets; love-letters

SCENE 4

On stage: No props required

Off stage: Coffin (**Chorus Men**)

SCENE 5

On stage: No props required

SCENE 6

On stage: Dustpan and brush

Off stage: Canoe (**Keith**)

SCENE 7

On stage: *No props required*

SCENE 8

On stage: *No props required*

Off stage: Pints of ale (**Company**)

SCENE 9

On stage: Radio

Personal: Pools coupon (**Keith**)
              Piece of paper and pen (**George**)

SCENE 10

On stage: Champagne

Off stage: Giant-sized cheque (**Bruce Forsyth**)

Personal: **Photographers**: Cameras

ACT II

SCENE 1

On stage: Pub bar. *Behind bar*: bottles of drink, beer pumps, etc.
              Banner reading "Welcome home Viv and Keith"
              Big sack of mail
              Pint glasses and drinks, etc. for the **Company**

Off stage: Pink Chevrolet Impala car

Personal: Bar bill (**Landlady**)

SCENE 2

On stage: Lawn-mowers

Personal: **Bank Manager**: documents and pen

Furniture and Property List

When the lights close in around Keith and Young Viv on page 46

Strike: Lawn-mowers

Set: Party drinks in interior of **Young Viv** and **Keith**'s home

Off stage: Drinks trolley (**Stewardess**)
Bags (**Doorman**)

When the lights close in around Keith and Young Viv on page 48

Strike: Party drinks

Set: New York hotel room settings: *including*: television, mini-bar

Scene 3

On stage: No additional props required

Scene 4

On stage: No props required

Off stage: Cup of tea and a whisky (**Florrie**)
Canary in a cage (**Keith**)

Scene 5

On stage: No props required

Scene 6

On stage: No props required

Off stage: Rails of dresses and other clothes shop objects (**Company**)

Scene 7

On stage: No props required

Personal: **Company in Salon Mystique**: beauty masks

LIGHTING PLOT

Practical fittings required: neon sign, television flicker effect

ACT I, SCENE 1

To open: Interior lighting on Salon Mystique. Spotlight on Viv throughout

Cue 1	**Viv**: " ... what it felt like ..." *Lighting change*	(Page 4)

ACT I, SCENE 2

To open: Exterior lighting on Castleford Street

Cue 2	**Young Viv** exits *Lighting change*	(Page 5)

ACT I, SCENE 3

To open: Interior lighting; light practical neon sign

Cue 3	**Young Viv** and **Matt** exit *Lighting change*	(Page 7)

ACT I, SCENE 4

To open: General exterior lighting

Cue 4	**Viv**: "... but still got caught in the middle." *Bring up interior lighting*	(Page 11)
Cue 5	**Young Viv** and **Matt** begin to make love *Lighting change*	(Page 14)

ACT I, SCENE 5

To open: The same; immediately following

Cue 6	**Young Viv**: (*singing*) " ... him again." *Lighting change*	(Page 17)

Lighting Plot

ACT I, SCENE 6

To open: General exterior lighting

Cue 7	**Keith**: "Hallo, love." *Lighting change*	(Page 19)

ACT I, SCENE 7

To open: The same, immediately following   (Page 19)

Cue 8	**Keith**: (*singing*) " Oh, the girl next door." *Lighting change*	(Page 21)

ACT I, SCENE 8

To open: Dance hall interior lighting

Cue 9	**Young Viv** and **Keith** move away from the other dancers *Lighting changes to night-time effect on* **Young Viv** *and* **Keith**	(Page 22)
Cue 10	**Viv**: "Pie and ale in't *Miners' Arms*." *Lighting change*	(Page 24)
Cue 11	**Miners/Wives**: (*singing*) "... do any good." *Fade lighting on* **Miners** *and* **Wives.** *Focus lighting on* **Keith** *and* **Young Viv**	(Page 26)

ACT I, SCENE 9

To open: Full interior lighting

Cue 12	**George/Keith**: (*singing*) " — two rooms." *Fade interior lighting. Spotlight on Viv remains*	(Page 31)

ACT I, SCENE 10

To open: Full bright interior lighing

No cues

ACT II, SCENE 1

To open: Interior pub lighting. Spotlight on Viv remaining throughout

Cue 13	**George** dumps the sack of mail *Close lights in on* **Keith, Young Viv** *and* **George**	(Page 39)

Cue 14	**Young Viv** and **Keith** begin to open some letters Bring up tight spotlight on **Granny/Fraudster**	(Page 39)
Cue 15	The **Fraudster** exits Fade spotlight; restore full interior state	(Page 39)
Cue 16	**Viv**: (*singing*) " Playing a trick?" Close lights in around **Young Viv** and **Keith**	(Page 42)

ACT I, SCENE 2

To open: The same, immediately following

Cue 17	**Young Viv**: "We can hardly wait." Lighting on interior of new Garforth home. Exterior effect on surrounding area	(Page 43)
Cue 18	**Keith/Young Viv/Viv**: "... unhappy with us!" Close lighting in on **Keith** and **Young Viv**	(Page 46)
Cue 19	The **Bank Manager** exits Bring up interior lighting on Garforth home	(Page 46)
Cue 20	The **Party Guests** exit Close lighting in on **Keith** and **Young Viv**	(Page 48)
Cue 21	A **Doorman** enters Interior lighting comes up on hotel room	(Page 49)
Cue 22	**Keith** switches on the television Bring up television flicker effect	(Page 49)

ACT II, SCENE 3

To open: The same, immediately following

Cue 23	**Young Viv**: (*singing*) " Drinking in America." Fade lights on main scene. Spotlight remains on **Viv**	(Page 51)

ACT II, SCENE 4

To open: The same

Cue 24	**Viv**: (*singing*) "... bottom of a glass." Bring up interior lights on **Young Viv** in her bedroom	(Page 51)
Cue 25	**Keith** exits Fade lights on main scene. Spotlight remains on **Viv**	(Page 53)

Lighting Plot   77

Cue 26	A **Policeman** enters *Bring up interior lighting on* **Young Viv** *and* **Policeman**	(Page 53)
Cue 27	The **Policeman** exits *Full exterior lighting comes up*	(Page 54)

ACT II, SCENE 5

To open: The same, immediately following

Cue 28	**Viv**: (*singing*) "Pieces of me." *Fade lights on Company. Bring up spotlight on Judge*	(Page 60)
Cue 29	**Viv**: " A brand new husband!" *Lighting change. Cut spotlight on Judge*	(Page 60)

ACT II, SCENE 6

To open: Lighting on **Young Viv** and **Husband 3**

Cue 30	**Viv**: " Was it 'eck!" *Lighting change*	(Page 62)
Cue 31	**Viv**: (*singing*) " I want my mate." *Dim lights and close in around* **Viv**	(Page 65)

ACT II, SCENE 7

To open: The same, immediately following

Cue 31	**Viv**: (*singing*) "... I see loomin'" *Bring up full interior lighting*	(Page 66)
Cue 32	The **Stranger** exits *Close lights in around* **Viv**	(Page 68)
Cue 33	**Viv**: "... me little story's ended." *Bring up full interior lights*	(Page 69)
Cue 34	**Viv**: "I wish, I wish!" *Fade lights on Salon Mystique. Light on front of the stage*	(Page 69)
Cue 35	**Viv**: "...when I had everything ..." *Black-out*	(Page 69)
Cue 37	When ready *Bring up full lighting for cast bows*	(Page 70)

EFFECTS PLOT

ACT I

No cues

ACT II

Cue 1   **Viv**: " ... happy in Garforth."   (Page 47)
Doorbell ring

www.ingramcontent.com/pod-product-compliance
Ingram Content Group UK Ltd.
Pitfield, Milton Keynes, MK11 3LW, UK
UKHW021845210426
5322IPUK00022B/470